Buddhist Psalms

By Shinran

Copyright © 2020 Lamp of Trismegistus. All rights reserved. No part of this publication may be reproduced or transmitted in any form or by any means, electronic or mechanical, including photocopying, recording, or by any information storage and retrieval system, without permission in writing from Lamp of Trismegistus. Reviewers may quote brief passages.

ISBN: 978-1-63118-465-9

Studies in Buddhism

Other Books in this Series and Related Titles

The Tree of Wisdom by Nagarjuna (978-1-63118-470-3)

The Path of Light: A Manual of Mahayana Buddhism by L. D. Barnett (978-1-63118-471-0)

Psalms of Solomon by King Solomon (978-1-63118-439-0)

The Old Past Master by Carl H. Claudy (978-1-63118-464-2)

Fortune-Telling by Playing Cards by Astra Cielo (978-1-63118-467-3)

The Rosicrucian Chemical Marriage by Christian Rosenkreuz (978-1-63118-458-1)

The Machinery of the Mind by Dion Fortune (978-1-63118-451-2)

Arcane Formulas or Mental Alchemy William Walker Atkinson (978-1-63118-459-8)

Magical Essays and Instructions by Florence Farr (978-1-63118-418-5)

The Human Aura: Astral Colors and Thought Forms William Walker Atkinson (978-1-63118-419-2)

Crystal Vision Through Crystal Gazing by Achad (978-1-63118-455-0)

American Indian Freemasonry by A. C. Parker (978-1-63118-460-4)

The Gospel of the Nativity of Mary by St. Matthew (978-1-63118-448-2)

Ghosts in Solid Form by Gambier Bolton (978-1-63118-469-7)

Thirty-One Hymns to the Star Goddess by Achad (978-1-63118-422-2)

Ancient Mysteries & Secret Societies by M. P. Hall (978-1-63118-410-9)

The Secrets of Enoch by Enoch (978-1-63118-449-9)

Audio Versions are also Available on Audible and iTunes

Table of Contents

Introduction...7

Lauding the Infinite One...15

Of Paradise...21

Concerning the Great Sutra...23

Concerning the Sutra of the Meditation...27

Concerning the Lesser Sutra...29

Of The Many Sutras Concerning the Infinite One...31

Concerning the Welfare of the Present World...33

Of Thanksgiving for Nagarjuna, the Great Teacher of India...37

Of Thanksgiving for Vasubandh, the Great Teacher of India...39

Of Thanksgiving for Donran, the Great Teacher of China...41

Concerning Unrighteous Deeds...47

Concerning Doshaku-Zenji...49

Concerning Zendo-Daishi...51

Concerning Genshin-Sozu...57

Concerning Hōnen Shōnin...59

Of the Three Periods...63

Concerning Belief and Doubt...73

In Praise of Prince Shotoku...77

Wherein with Lamentation I Make my Confession...79

Additional Psalms...83

INTRODUCTION

It is a singular fact that though many of the earlier Buddhist Scriptures have been translated by competent scholars, comparatively little attention has been paid to later Buddhist devotional writings, and this although the developments of Buddhism in China and Japan give them the deepest interest as reflecting the spiritual mind of those two great countries. They cannot, however, be understood without some knowledge of the faith which passed so entirely into their life that in its growth it lost some of its own infant traits and took on others, rooted, no doubt, in the beginnings in India, but expanded and changed as the features of the child may be forgotten in the face of the man and yet perpetuate the unbroken succession of heredity. It is especially true that Japan cannot be understood without some knowledge of the Buddhism of the Greater Vehicle (as the developed form is called), for it was the influence that molded her youth as a nation, that shaped her aspirations, and was the inspiration of her art, not only in the written word, but in every art and higher handicraftsman-ship that makes her what she is. Whatever centuries may pass or the future hold in store for her, Japan can never lose the stamp of Buddhism in her outer or her spiritual life.

The world knows little as yet of the soul of Mahayana Buddhism, though much of its outer observance, and for this reason a crucial injustice has been done in regarding it merely as a degraded form of the earlier Buddhism—a rank off-shoot of the teachings of the Gautama Buddha, a system of idolatry and priestly power from which the austere purity of the earlier faith has passed away.

The truth is that Buddhism, like Christianity, in every country where it has sowed its seed and reaped its harvest, developed along the lines indicated by the mind of that people. The Buddhism of Japan differs from that of Tibet as profoundly as the Christianity of Abyssinia from that of Scotland—yet both have conserved the essential principle.

Buddhism was not a dead abstraction, but a living faith, and it therefore grew and changed with the growth of the mind of man, enlarging its perception of truth. As in the other great faiths, the ascent of the Mount of Vision reveals worlds undreamed, and proclaims what may seem to be new truths, but are only new aspects of the Eternal. Japanese Buddhists still base their belief on the utterances of the Buddhas, but they have enlarged their conception of the truths so taught, and they hold that the new flower and fruit spring from the roots that were planted in dim ages before the Gautama Buddha taught in India, and have since rushed hundred-armed to the sun. Such is the religious history of mankind, and Buddhism obeys its sequence.

The development of Mahayana Buddhism from the teaching of the Gautama Buddha has been often compared with that of the Christian faith from the Jewish, but it may be better compared with the growth of a sacerdotal system from the simplicities of the Gospel of St. Mark. That the development should have been on the same lines in all essential matters of symbol and (in the most important respects) of doctrine, modified only by Eastern habits of thought and environment, is a miracle of coincidence which cannot be paralleled in the world unless it be granted that Christianity filtering along the great trade routes of an earlier world joined hands with Buddhism in many unsuspected ways and places. Evidence is accumulating that this is so, and in a measure at present almost incredible. And if it be so—if it be true that in spite of racial distinctions, differences of thought and circumstance, the religious thought of East and West has so many and so great meeting-points, the hope of the world in things spiritual may lie in the recognition of that fact and in a future union now shadowed forth only in symbol and in a great hope. This, however, is no essay on Buddhism, either earlier or later, and what I have said is necessary to the introduction of these Jodo-Wasan, or Psalms of the Pure Land, which are a part not only of the literature, but also of the daily worship and spiritual life of Japan. Their history may be briefly told.

Buddhism passed into Japan from China and Korea about 1,320 years ago, in or about the year 552 A.D. It adapted itself with perfect comprehension to the ideals of the Japanese people, inculcating among them the teachings of morality common to the great faiths with, in addition, the spiritual unction, the passion of love and sympathy, self-devotion, and compassion, in which Buddhism and Christianity are alike pre-eminent. The negative side of Buddhism, with its passionless calm and self-renunciation, is the only one that has been realized in the West, and the teachings of Mahayana which have borne fruit and flower, visible to all the world, of happiness, courtesy, kindliness in the spiritual attitude of a whole people, have never received the honor which was their due.

For with the Buddhist faith there came the germ of the belief that the Gautama Buddha in his own grandeur bore witness to One Greater—the Amitabha or Amida Buddha—that One who in boundless Light abides, life of the Universe, without color, without form, the Lover of man, his Protector and Refuge. He may, He must be worshipped, for in Him are all the essential attributes of Deity, and He, the Savior of mankind, has prepared a pure land of peace for his servants, beyond the storms of life and death. This belief eventually crystallized and became a dogma in the faith of the Pure Land, known in Japan as Jodo Shinshu, a faith held by the majority of the Japanese people. It is a belief which has spread also in Eastern Siberia, many parts of China, Hawaii, and, in fact, where-ever the Japanese race has spread. And the man who stated this belief for all time was Shinran Shonin, author of the Psalms here presented.

He was born in the year 1175 A.D. near City-Royal—Kyoto, the ancient capital of Japan. He was a son of one of the noblest families, in close connection with the Imperial House, and had it not been for the passion for truth and the life of the spirit which consumed him, his history would have been that of the many other brilliant young men who sank into mere courtiers "Dwellers above the Clouds," as the royalties and courtiers of the day were called among the people. But the clear air above the clouds in which his spirit spread its wings was not that of City-Royal, and the Way opened before him as it has opened before many a saint of the Christian Church, for while still a child he lost both his parents, and so, meditating on the impermanence of mortal life, and seeing how the fashion of this world passes away, he abandoned his title and became a monk in one of the noble monasteries whose successors still stand glorious among the pine woods above Lake Biwa.

These were not only monasteries, but seats of learning, as in Europe in the Middle Ages, and here the Doctrines were subjected to brilliant analysis and logical subtleties which had almost superseded the living faith. In that cold atmosphere the spirit of Shiran Shonin could not spread its wings, though for twenty years he gave his thoughts to its empty glitter. Therefore, at the age of twenty-nine he cast it all behind him, and in deep humility cast himself at the feet of the great Teacher Honen, who, in the shades of Higashiyama, was setting forth the saving power of the Eternal

One who abides in the Light and in whom is no darkness—the Buddha of Boundless Light. And in this place and from this man Shinran received enlightenment.

Life now lay before him as a problem. Unlike as the two men are in character and methods, his position resembled that of Martin Luther on quitting the Church of Rome. For the Buddhist monastic rule requires its members to be homeless, celibate, vegetarian, and here, like Luther, Shinran joined issue with them. To his mind the attainment of man lay in the harmonious development of body and spirit, and in the fulfilment, not the negation of the ordinary human duties. Accordingly, in his thirty-first year, after deep consideration, he married the daughter of Prince Kujo Kanezane, Chief Minister of the Emperor and head of one of the greatest houses in Japan, and in that happy union he tasted four years of simple domestic joy, during which a son was born to him. Then the storm broke.

Trouble was stirred up by the orthodox Buddhist Church with evil reports which reached the ears of the Emperor, and Shinran was sent into banishment in the lonely and primitive province of Echigo—a terrible alternative for a man of noble birth and refined culture. He took it, however, with perfect serenity as a mission to those untaught and neglected people, and into their darkness he brought the light of the Father of Lights, and the people flocked to the warmth and wonder of the new hope, and heard him gladly. The story is told by a contemporary, whom I have thus rendered :

"In the spring of the third year of the era of Kennin, the age of Shinran Shonin was twenty-nine. Driven by the desire for seclusion, he departed to the monastery of Yoshimizu. For as his day was so remote from the era of the Lord Buddha, and the endurance of man in the practice of religious austerity was now weakened, he would fain seek the one broad, straight way that is now made plain before us, leaving behind him the more devious and difficult roads in which he had a long time wandered. For so it was that Honen Shonin, the great teacher of the Doctrine of the Land of Pure Light, had taught him plainly of the inmost heart of the Faith, raising up in him the firm foundation of that teaching. Therefore he certainly received at that time the true meaning of the Divine Promise of universal salvation, and attained unto the imperishable faith by which alone the ignorant can enter into Nirvana without condition or price.

"From the province of Echigo Shinran passed onward to that of Hitachi, and entered into seclusion at Inada, that little village of the region of Kasama. Very lonely was his dwelling, yet many disciples sought after him, and though the humble door of the monastery was closed against them, many nobles and lesser persons thronged into the village. So his hope of spreading abroad the Holy Teaching was fulfilled and his desire to bring joy to the people was satisfied. Thus he declared that the revelation vouchsafed to him in the Temple of Rokkaku by the Bodhisattwa of Pity was indeed made manifest."

It is that revelation which speaks in these Psalms—the love, aspiration, passion for righteousness and humility which are the heart of all the great religious utterances of the world.

"Alas for me, Shinran, the ignorant exile who sinks into the deeps of the great ocean of human affections, who toils to climb the high mountains of worldly prosperity, and is neither glad to be with them who return no more to illusion, nor takes delight in approaching more nearly to true enlightenment. O the pity of it ! O the shame of it!"

This cry alternates with the joy of perfect aspiration, and it is that which keeps these psalms in warm human touch with the spirituality that is neither of race nor time, but for eternity.

He was sixty-two years of age when he returned from exile to City-Royal, and though he made it his center, it was his home no more. He wandered from place to place, teaching as he went, after the manner of the Buddhas. At the age of ninety his strength suddenly failed, and the next day he passed away in perfect peace.

Such were the outward events of his life; his own writings must give the history of his soul. His teachings to-day are spread far and wide in the land of his birth, and are an inspiration to millions within and without its shores. In him was the harmonized spirit of Buddhism at its highest. Those who can enter into the heart of Shinran Shonin will have gained understanding of the heart of a mighty people which is said to be impossible of Western reading, and yet in its essentials is simple as the heart of a child.

LAUDING THE INFINITE ONE

Since He who is Infinite attained unto the Wisdom Supreme, the long, long ages of ten Kalpas have rolled away.

The Light of His Dharma-Kaya is in this world eyes to the blind.

Seek refuge in the True Illumination! For the light of His Wisdom is infinite.

In all the worlds there is nothing upon which His light shines not.

Take refuge in the Light universal.

As the Light of His deliverance is boundless, he who is within it is freed from the lie of affirmation or denial.

Seek refuge in That which is beyond understanding,

For His glory is all-embracing as the air. It shineth and pierces all things, and there is nothing hid from the light thereof.

Take refuge in the ultimate Strength, for His pure radiance is above all things. He who perceives this Light is set free from the fetters of Karma.

Seek refuge in the World-Honored.

Since His glorious radiance is above all He is called the Buddha of Divine Light. And by Him is the darkness of the three worlds Enlightened.

Excellent is the Light of His Wisdom. Therefore is he called the Buddha of Clear Shining.

He who is within the Light, being washed from the soil of Karma, shall attain unto the final deliverance.

Take refuge in the Mighty Consoler. Wheresoever His mercy shineth throughout all the worlds, men rejoice in its gladdening light.

The darkness of ignorance perishes before His light. Therefore is He hailed as the Buddha of Radiant Wisdom. All the Buddhas and the threefold choir of sages praise Him.

His glory shineth for ever and ever. Therefore is He called the Buddha of Everlasting Light.

Most excellent is the virtue of this light, for he who perceives it is born into Paradise without dissolution of being.

The glory of the Infinite is boundless, therefore is He known as the Buddha of Light Past Comprehension.

All the Buddhas glorify the majesty of His holiness that leadeth all the earth into His Kingdom.
His clear shining transcends all revelation, nor can human speech utter it. Therefore is He named the Buddha of Light Unspeakable.

All the Buddhas glorify the glory of the Infinite One who is Buddha through His promise of Light immeasurable.

Take refuge in Him who is Holiest of Holy. Sun and moon are lost in the ocean of His splendor. Therefore is He named that Infinite in whose radiance Sun and Moon are darkened. Before whose Divine Power even that Buddha made flesh in India himself falters in ascribing praise to the Majesty of His true glory.

Far beyond human numbering are the wise in the high assemblage of the Infinite One. Therefore let him who would be born into the Land of Purity seek refuge in the Great Congregation.

In Paradise are the Mighty unnumbered, Bodhisattvas ranked in that hierarchy nearest to the Perfect Enlightenment. Thence are they made flesh upon earth according to the way of salvation that all having life might be saved.

Take refuge in the ocean-deep Soul Universal.

For the sake of all dwelling in the Ten Regions hath He kept the fullness of all the Teachings, in His divine and mighty promises.

He who is Infinite never rests, for together with the Bodhisattvas of Compassion and Pure Reason He labors, that the souls of them that duly receive Him may have salvation, enlightening them with the light of His mercy.

When he who is born into the land of Pure Peace returns again into this sinful world, even like unto that Buddha made flesh in India, he wearies not in seeking the welfare of all men.

Seek refuge in the World-Honored, for His Divine Dower is Almighty and beyond man's measure, being made perfect in inconceivable Holiness.

The Sravakas, the Bodhisattvas, the Heavenly Beings and Souls in Paradise, they in whom wisdom is made equal unto beauty, declare their attributes in order, according to their former birth.

Seek refuge in Him in whom all strengths are equal.

Naught is there to compare with the excellent beauty of the Souls in Paradise, for their being is infinite as space, and far are they above celestials and mortal man.

Whoso would be born into Paradise shall in this life be made one with those men that return no more unto birth and death.

In that Pure Land is none who hath stood among doubting men, and none also who hath trusted in his own deeds for Salvation. To this do all the Buddhas witness.

If all having life in the Ten Regions hear this Holiest Name of Him that is Infinite, and attain unto the true faith, they shall obtain joy and gladness.

For when a man with joy accepts the sacred vow of Him that is infinite who saith, "I will not attain unto perfect Enlightenment unless in Me shall all the world be made whole," at that very time he shall assuredly be born into Paradise.

Seek refuge in the Almighty Spirit.

By the divine might of His promise, by the Infinite One was Paradise created; yea, and the Souls of men that dwell therein. And there is naught that may compare with them.

Seek refuge in the unutterable Wisdom.

Of His Land of Peace the half cannot be told. Even the word of the Buddha himself could not utter it.

Myriads of happy souls were born, are born and shall be born into that Land of Purity, not from this world alone, but from the hidden worlds also, and the Ten Regions.

So soon as man heareth the holy name of the Infinite One and with great gladness praises him, he shall attain to the reward of the holy Treasury of Merit.

Go forward, O Valiant Souls, seeking the Law though all the worlds fall into flame and ruin, for ye shall have passed beyond birth and death!

The innumerable Buddhas praise the triumphant divinity of the Bringer of Light. To Him do gather the myriad Bodhisattvas, unnumbered as the Sands of Ganges in worship from the Eastern world.

As from the East, so gather also to the Infinite One the Bodhisattvas from the Nine Regions of the worlds.

With Sacred Psalms the Gautama Buddha himself lauds the boundless glory of the Infinite One.

Seek refuge in the World-Honored. To Him do the myriad Buddhas of the ten Regions bring homage with songs and praises, that they may sow the seeds of merit.

Bring homage to the Hall of Great Teaching and to the living Bo tree that is in Paradise! Yet this land, glorious with the Holy Tree, radiant with the Hall of Great Teaching that shineth with the Seven Jewels, where innumerable souls hastening from all the ends of the Earth shall be born, is but the temporal Paradise.

In awful reverence seek refuge in the purity of Him that welcomes. For by His Divine Promise was this glorious land, great beyond human measurement, made to be.

Seek refuge in the wisdom inconceivable. For the perfection of His Virtue—that Virtue availing for all the world, and the perfect way by which He wills that man shall take refuge in Him, are past all human speech or thought.

Take refuge in the wisdom that is most truly infinite. For He is faithful, having promised in His Divine Might, and on his perfect clear promise that cannot be shaken is the merciful way of salvation built.

OF PARADISE

Seek refuge in the heavenly harmony.

For the jewel groves and gem trees of Paradise give forth a sweet and most excellent melody in pure and ordered unison.

Seek refuge in the Divine Promise, the Treasury of Merit,

For the seven jewel trees are fragrant in Paradise where the flowers, the fruits, the branches and the leaves thereof

Cast back their radiance the one to the other.

Bring homage to the perfect Righteousness. As the pure wind blows over the trees glorious with jewels,

It draws from them a noble music with fivefold strains of harmony.

In all the world is no place hidden from the glory shed by hundreds of myriad rays from the heart of every flower of Paradise.

Like unto a golden mountain reflecting the myriad rays of these heavenly blossoms, so is the form of the Infinite One.

From His Sacred Body, as from a wellspring, flows this light over the Ten Regions of the world.

By His Sacred teaching He leadeth all having life into the way of light.

Seek refuge in the Treasury of Righteousness.

For in Paradise is that holy lake, with its waters of eightfold Virtue, all-glorious with the seven jewels. And all this is the inconceivable handiwork of Purity.

Seek refuge in the All-Honored.

For when sorrow and sighing are fled away, the Holy Land shall rejoice with joy and singing. Therefore is it called Paradise.

The Buddhas of the Three Ages and the Ten Regions, they in whom the Dual Wisdom is perfect and their illumination entire, lead all the worlds marvelously into the way of Salvation, the Truth being their Vehicle.

He that seeks refuge in the Kingdom of the Infinite One is a citizen of the Kingdom of every Buddha.

Let him that is set free, with single heart give praises unto One Buddha, for in so doing he praises all.

The faithful believer at that moment when he rejoices in the sound of the name of the Infinite One hath revealed unto his very eyes the Buddha of Light.

Let him that hath faith praise the Virtue of the Divine Wisdom.

Let him strive to declare it unto all men that he may offer his thankfulness for the grace of the Buddha.

CONCERNING THE GREAT SUTRA

The Venerable Ananda, rising from his seat, and looking upwards to the World-Honored Gautama Buddha, his eyes being opened, marveled greatly, seeing the glory of his Lord so transfigured.

The Venerable Ananda asked the Cause of that glory, for the Lord, shining in the Light that was hitherto unseen of the world, taught openly, for the first time, that Truth for which He came into the world.

In the meditation of the Great Calm the Buddha whose countenance is glorious, commends the most excellent wisdom of Ananda for that he asked the way of knowledge, desiring to be instructed.

That Buddha that was made flesh in India was in this world manifested that he might preach the Divine Promise of Him who is Infinite.

Hard is it to see the hidden blossom of the myriad-century-blooming Lotus, so hard also is it for a man's understanding to receive the message of that Blessed One.

Ten Kalpas of Ages have rolled away since He who is Infinite attained unto the Wisdom, yet before the myriads of the Kalpas He was.

He who is of the Light Ineffable, Holiest Refuge of men, ordaining that His saving grace should be made manifest, duly considered all the worlds of the Ten Regions, under the guidance of the holy Buddha of Loka-is-Vara-Raja.

Purity, Rejoicing, Wisdom, these three are the Supernal Essence of the light of the Infinite One that enlightens all things, communicating good to all the worlds of the Ten Regions.

Teaching all that have life in the Ten Regions, that they might, with sincerity, faith, and hope, be born again into Paradise, He set forth that promise infinite and divine—the true seed of birth within the Kingdom of Truth.

Whoso attains unto the True Faith is in unity with them that return no more to birth and death, for having thus attained, they pass onward into Nirvana, their lives being ended.

In His great compassion the Blessed One accomplished His infinite wisdom in His divine promise, ordaining that womanhood shall be raised into manhood.

Instructing all that have life in the Ten Regions how they should through sincerity, effort, and hope be born into the Temporal Paradise, He faithfully promises to manifest Himself unto the eyes of the dying, opening wide the gate of all righteousness before them.

By the divine promise to the dying of His consoling presence our Lord instructs men that they shall make to grow all righteousness revealed in the Sutra of Meditation upon the Buddha of Infinite Life.

All righteous deeds done of men in true obedience to the holy Doctrine of Sincerity and right-doing, are but the seed of merit that shall be born within the Temporal Paradise.

Instructing All that have life in the Ten Regions how that they may through sincerity, merit, and hope be born into the Temporal Paradise, He promises that no man shall lose salvation, for He hath opened the Gate of Truth.

By the Divine Promise of the final salvation hath our Lord instructed the men of the Single Vehicle to recite His Holy Name that is the Essence of all the merit revealed in the Lesser Sutra of the Buddha of Infinite Life.

He that recites the Holy name by his own effort and in the mind of meditation or of dispersing, being led by the virtue of the divine promise of final salvation, turns naturally in at the Gate of Truth.

He that holds not the True Faith, even though he desire to be born into the Pure Paradise of Joy, must go unto his own place, and it shall be in the border of the Outermost Places, for this is the fruit of doubting the mystery of the Supreme Wisdom.

That a man should be a Buddha, made manifest in this world, is a rare thing and difficult. So difficult is it also to hear the excellent doctrine of all the Buddhas and Bodhisattvas. In all the myriads of Kalpas such a way comes seldom.

Difficult is it for men to find a wise Teacher; so is it also for them to be instructed and to hear the Holy Law. More difficult still is it to receive the True Faith.

More difficult is it for men to receive the Divine Promise made unto men than to receive all other teachings.

The Lord Buddha teaches that this is of all hard things most difficult and yet again more difficult.

The true Doctrine teaches men that they may become Buddhas in reciting the Holy Name, and so therefore is it that all other faiths and moralities are but transitory doorways unto the Truth. Man comprehends not that Pure Land of Peace unless he holds fast the true Doctrine, casting aside that which is transitory.

Seek refuge in the Sole Vehicle of His merciful promise. For the transitory teachings have let and hindered men in the Way of Enlightenment so that they must needs pass through the long weariness of births and deaths.

CONCERNING THE SUTRA OF THE MEDITATION

That Lord that was made flesh in India, the Lord of great pity, showing unto Vaidehi, Queen of Magadha, the golden mirror created by his marvelous power, commanded her to choose the Land of Pure Joy among all the worlds therein appearing.

Binbisara, he who commanded that an ascetic should be slain before his pre-ordained time was come, by his own son was imprisoned in a seven-walled prison as the due recompense of his violence.

Ajāta-Šatru, prince and heir of Magadha, denouncing his mother as a traitor, with drawn sword ran furiously upon her.

Then said Jīvaka the minister and another with him: "This act is worthy only of an outcast. For the fame of our race unworthy art thou to dwell in the Palace." And earnestly did they counsel him to change his evil purpose.

Laying his hand on his sword-hilt, Jīvaka, the minister, drew backwards a few steps, steadfastly regarding the prince, that he might avert this great sin. And so it was that the prince laid down his sword, and secluded his mother in a palace.

Certain is it that Ananda with Vaidehi, Devadatta and yet others, bearing their part in this great sorrow of the royal palace of Magadha, must needs so suffer that they might know the infinite pity of the Blessed One, that Lord who in this world made manifest the true teaching.

And all these wise ones having so received instruction revealed unto us, who are of all evil-doers worst, the true way, the refuge of His divine promise that absolves all the sins of men.

For when the full time was come that by the will of our Lord and of Vaidehi the teaching of the Pure Land should be made known here on Earth, Ajāta-Šatru, her son, sinned this sin, Varshakara his minister bearing testimony against it.

It is needful that the heart of a man be opened unto the Faith universal which He who is Blessed hath shown us, forsaking the belief that his own works shall save him, for in every man the power to perform righteous deeds is differing.

CONCERNING THE LESSER SUTRA

The Eternal Father is called the Buddha of Infinite Light, because very mightily He holds in safety all beings dwelling in the Ten Regions of the world who, by His merciful enlightenment, recite His Holy Name.

The myriad Buddhas, unnumbered as the sands of Ganges, counsel all having life to trust in the Supernal Virtue of the Holy Name, declaring that weighed against this, even righteous deeds are the lesser good.

The innumerable Buddhas, countless as the sands of Ganges, are a testimony and a shield to all that have life in this sorrowful and sinful world, declaring unto them that teaching most high and difficult of acceptance, which is the true faith.

Whoso attains unto a Soul clear and enduring as diamond shall testify unto his thankfulness for the limitless grace of the Blessed One, for even the testimony and the safeguarding that he hath of all the Buddhas proceed only from the fulfilment of His most merciful promise.

The innumerable Buddhas, countless as the sands of Ganges, guide into a sure trust in the Holy Name those sinful creatures and evil-hearted that wander in the darkness of this wicked world bearing the five signs of degeneration upon it.

OF THE MANY SUTRAS CONCERNING THE INFINITE ONE

Having great pity, our Eternal Father lightens the dark night of ignorance, manifesting Himself in that Land of Joy as the Buddha of Infinite Light which enlightens all the worlds with its immeasurable glory.

That Lord most compassionate, the Buddha of immeasurable Light, He who had attained unto the Supreme Wisdom even before the myriads of Kalpas were, pitying them that know not, made himself manifest in the Palace of Kapila as the Lord Sakya-muni.

If a man had the duration of all the myriad Kalpas, had he innumerable tongues and each of these tongues innumerable voices, yet should he vainly essay the praises of that Blessed One.

The Lord instructs us that the way into Paradise is straight and easy. Therefore whoso receives not this Truth is, in verity, called a man that hath not eyes to see nor ears to hear.

The One true freedom is the Highest, and the Absolute is perfect freedom. And when we attain unto that freedom, for us shall desire and doubt vanish away.

When every man is beloved of us, even as the son of our own body, there is the Universal Mind made perfect in us. And this shall be in Paradise.

He who is in all things supreme, is Himself Nirvana, and Nirvana is that true light that abides in the Land that is to come, but this world cannot know it.

Our Lord instructs us that he who rejoices in his faith is, in so doing, in unity with the Highest. For true faith is the seed of light, and the seed of true light is in itself the potentiality of that which is Deity.

Whoso trusts not in the Supreme Wisdom of the Enlightened One, clinging unto his own purblind knowledge, must suffer by fire for long Kalpas of ages.

CONCERNING THE WELFARE OF THE PRESENT WORLD

He that hath unending pity, the Buddha of Infinite Life, hath given unto us in the Sutra of Golden Light a teaching concerning long life, that the way of long life and the welfare of the people might be made known unto them.

Dengyo-Daishi, he who taught the Tendaishu in the mount of Hiye, hath compassionately instructed us that we should recite Namuamidabutsu, that Holiest Name, as a sure shield against the seven sorts of calamities.

Whoso recites the Holy Name, that is higher than all other virtues, shall be set free from the fetters of the past, the present, and the future.

To him that recites the Holy Name shall be good unending even in this world, for the sin of his former births is vanquished and his youth set free from death.

To him that recites the Holy Name, shall Brahma and Chakra the great king bring homage, and about him shall heavenly beings and benignant deities keep watch throughout the days and nights.

That man that recites the Holy Name shall the four mighty Regents in Heaven guard through the days and nights against the disturbance of all evil spirits.

To him that recites the Holy Name shall the Deity of the Earth bring homage, watching over him throughout the day and night, as the shadow follows its substance.

To him who recites the Holy Name, Nanda and Upananda the Naga Kings, together with their attendant deities shall bring homage, watching over him throughout the day and night.

To him who recites the Holy Name, the King of Death, together with his ministers in the five worlds, shall do reverence, guarding him throughout the days and nights.

Mara, the Tempter, he who is Ruler of that heaven where pleasures are collected, hath sworn unto the Lord to shield him from temptation who recites the Holy Name.

All good deities in Earth and Heaven shall be gracious unto him who recites the Holy Name, shielding him throughout the days and nights.

All evil spirits in heaven and earth tremble before that believer who stands upon the Immutable promise. For even in this world hath he the mind of Divine Illumination.

Kwannon and Seishi, the Bodhisattvas of incarnate Pity and Wisdom, together with their companions, innumerable as the sands of Ganges, shall be beside him who recites the Holy Name, even as the shadow cleaves to the substance.

Within the Light of Buddha of Infinite Light are unnumbered Buddhas, and of these, each and every one shall shield him who hath within him the true Faith.

Whoso recites the Holy Name shall be surrounded himself by those Buddhas who cannot be numbered, who in the Ten Regions with joy protect and guide him.

Upon the Sutra of Suraigama-Samadhi, I, Shinran Shōnin, have uttered these eight lauds praising the virtue of Seishi the Bodhisattva of Wisdom.

Seishi, he who is the Bodhisattva of Wisdom, having comprehended the fullness of the Holiest Name, rising from his seat, prostrated himself beneath the feet of our Lord, worshipping Him, he and his fellowship, and thus he spoke:

"O my Lord, in the ancient time, before the Kalpas innumerable as the sands of Ganges, there was manifest in this world a Buddha, and His Name was called—The Buddha of Infinite Light.

"In His footsteps twelve Buddhas followed, and twelve long Kalpas have rolled away. And of these Buddhas the last was He that is called that Buddha in whose glory the Sun and Moon are even as darkness.

"Unto me hath that Buddha revealed the Path of the meditation of the Supreme—that meditation wherein He instructs us that all the Buddhas of all the Ten Regions compassionate as even as a father pities his child.

Whoso seeks refuge in Buddha, as a child in the bosom of his mother shall verily perceive Him now or in the time that shall be. And it shall be soon.

"As a man encompassed by the cloud of incense casts sweet odors about him, so he that trusts in the Holy Promise is spiritually endued with the Divine Essence.

"When I was initiate in right doing, I attained unto the high way of that assurance that freed me from birth and death, through the teaching of the Noble Doctrine of the Holy Name.

"Therefore in this world, rejoicing, I guide the faithful believer into the way of Purity."

Now with all praise let us give thanks unto the merciful goodness of the Bodhisattva of Wisdom.

OF THANKSGIVING FOR NAGARJUNA, THE GREAT TEACHER OF INDIA

Nagarjuna, the great teacher, setting forth in many excellent writings the praise of the Kingdom of Purity, hath instructed us to recite the Holy Name.

For the Lord Buddha declared in prophecy that in India, in the Southern Parts, should arise a great Teacher, trampling upon the false teachings of affirmation and denial.

Nagarjuna, the Great Teacher, he who mightily set forth the noble doctrine of the greater Vehicle, and himself attained unto that height whereon a man rejoices eternally in the Faith, hath very sweetly persuaded men that they should receive the teaching of the Holy Name.

Nagarjuna, that great priest, setting forth the two ways—the way that is straight and plain, and the way of high austerity, leadeth very gently to the Ark of the Divine Promise such as are driven through the weariness of births and deaths.

He who receives this teaching of Nagarjuna the Great Teacher, should recite always the Holy Name, believing the Divine Promise of the Buddha of Infinite Light.

Whoso would quickly attain unto that resting-place where illusion ceases, should recite the Holy Name holding his mind in steadfast piety.

One Ark only, that Ark of the Divine Promise of our merciful Father, doth voyage and bear us unto the shore of the eternal peace—even us who so long have drifted hither and thither in the ocean of birth and death.

This great priest hath in one utterance set forth that the Lord is Ruler indeed of the sacred teaching, and that herein are the holy Bodhisattvas His ministers. Therefore should we bring homage unto our Lord.

The mighty company of the Bodhisattvas utter these words, "When we became wise in holiness, yea, we who have striven through Kalpas unnumbered,

"Yet could we not root out our earthly desires which are the very seed of birth and death. But through that only way of the meditation of the Highest did we attain unto the final deliverance that hath destroyed all our sin."

OF THANKSGIVING FOR VASUBANDH, THE GREAT TEACHER OF INDIA

Among those doctrines taught of our Lord Vasubandh, the great priest hath persuaded us who are full of sinful desires to accept the Divine Promise of our infinite Father.

Only to Him who is above all things is known the glory of the Land of Peace. Wide as the sky and boundless is it spread forth.

Whoso believeth in the power of the Divine Promise shall verily be at one with the holy Essence, even as the turbid stream is clear and pure within the ocean depth when they have flowed together.

When the assemblage of the believers in the holy faith is born within that Land of Purity that hath sprung from the lotus of the true enlightenment, soon shall their heart's desire be fulfilled in them.

The heavenly spirits and those souls freed from illusion, they who are born in the land of purity from the wisdom deep as the ocean of the Divine Promise, differ not the one from the other in their powers. Pure are they as the air is pure.

Vasubandh, that exalted master of excelling works, who himself hath found refuge in the Buddha of Infinite Light, hath declared that whoso is borne in the Vehicle of the Divine Promise shall without doubt attain unto the Promised Land.

Whoso taketh refuge in the Buddha of Infinite Light, that light that shineth unto all the worlds of the Ten Regions, shall be called, according to the teaching of that master of excelling works, a man whose heart is great, and to him shall the True Light be shown.

He whose heart is great and who shall attain unto the true enlightenment is he also that desires the salvation of all living, and verily the true faith given of that Blessed One is salvation.

The single heart perceives the true faith, and so doing is strong and clear as the diamond, and this strength is the wisdom of the supreme that strengthens us.

When we shall attain unto the Promised Land, which is that Nirvana past all understanding, there shall we labor abundantly for the salvation of all living things. For so the Sutra teaches us in these words: "A heart that inclines to the succor of others."

OF THANKSGIVING FOR DONRAN, THE GREAT TEACHER OF CHINA

Donran, that great teacher of China, being instructed of Bodhi-ruci, the priest of India, sought refuge in the Land of Purity, and thus doing he burned with fire the books of the Taoist teaching which he had aforetime held in honor.

Having thus cast from him the writings that he had so many years diligently studied, he preached unto all men the doctrine of the Divine Promise, and, so teaching, he led men that are fast bound in the fetters of illusion, in at the Gate of the Great Peace.

A mighty King of this world brought homage unto him in his monastery and put unto him this question, saying: "If so it is that the Land of Purity should be in all the Ten Regions, how then is it declared unto us in the Sutra that it is in the Western Heaven?"

And with humble piety he replied:

"Of this matter can I not tell thee. It is too high for me. Still am I in the lower rank of wisdom, even still small is my knowledge. I cannot fathom this great mystery."

All men in the priesthood or the people who know not the rock of their trust, did Donran the Great Priest guide unto the sure refuge of the doctrine of the Land of Bliss.

He abode in the Temple of the Great Rock, being favorably bidden thereto by the King of the Gi Dynasty, and in the evening of his days he travelled into the district of Dun.

And this King of the Gi Dynasty reverently offered unto him the holy title of Shinran (Ran of Divinity) and the honorable name of "Rock of the Venerable Ran"—that his dwelling-place should be called by it.

Great and mighty upon the people was his spiritual power in the temple of Genchu and in the fourth year of Kokwa of the Gi Dynasty the Temple of Yosen became his beloved dwelling.

And when he had reached sixty-seven years, he sought his final refuge in the Eternal Kingdom. And at that departing were vouchsafed many holy marvels unto which all men, both of the priests and people; came and did reverence.

And when Donran the Great High Priest had departed into the Peace, the King of the Gi Dynasty by a royal order commanded there should be built for him a holy monument in the lands of Dun.

What man could know the unsearchable mystery of the faith and deeds of the Divine Promise were it not for that most excelling commentary of Donran the wise Priest, which he wrote concerning the teaching of Vasubandh that had lived aforetime.

He who believeth that the Sole Vehicle of the Divine Promise, most perfect, most mighty, receives within itself the Greatest of Sinners, and this because it is its chief will so to do, will receive the depth of this essential teaching—namely, that before the eyes of the Instructed, illusion and wisdom are in their Essence One.

Among the Five Mysteries that are preached in this Sutra, the mystery of the Divine Power of the Enlightened One is highest, and this is the holy vow of our Blessed One, this and this only.

Unto us hath our Father given those two spiritual gifts. Of these the first is the Virtue whereby we attain unto His Kingdom, and the second is the Virtue whereby having so attained we return into this world for the Salvation of men. By the merit of these two gifts are we initiates of the true faith and of its deeds.

When we shall have attained unto the faith and the deeds of the Merciful Promise through our Father that is in all things able to give them unto us, birth and death are henceforward as Nirvana. And this is called the Gift of Departure.

And when we shall have attained unto that height which is desire for the ingathering of all beings into Paradise, shall we return again into this world that we may be Saviors of Men. And this is called the Gift of Returning.

That "Single Mind" expounded unto us by Vasubandh, the Master of Writings that excel, is nothing other than the faith of us that are now fast bound in illusion. So teaches Donran the Great Teacher in his Commentary.

The Buddha of that inexpressible Light that shineth into the worlds of the Ten Regions, being forever enlightened in the night of ignorance, hath most certainly opened the way of Nirvana to every man who even for one moment rejoices in receiving His Divine Promise.

By the merit of His Infinite Light, when we attain unto that faith divine and omnipotent, the ice of illusion shall melt into the water of perfect wisdom.

Sin is made one with virtue in its essence, even as ice is one with water. The more there is ice, so much the more water is there. So also is the binding up of sin with virtue.

In the unbounded ocean of the Holy Name is not seen even one single death of a blasphemer. For the myriad streams of sin are on purity with the ocean of righteousness when they have flowed into the impurity thereof.

When the streams of illusion have flowed into the Great Sea of the Merciful Promise of the Enlightened One, whose light shineth into all the worlds of the Ten Religions, then shall they too become the pure water of the Perfect Wisdom.

No other way is there of attaining unto the Perfect Enlightenment save only by birth into the Land of Gladness, and therefore have all the Enlightened Ones exhorted men that they should receive the Doctrine of the Kingdom Purity.

The Great Priest hath well taught us that in order to cleanse our deeds, words, and thoughts of deceitfulness, our Father hath performed the three of His pure and universal.

There is no way unto the Kingdom of Gladness save only by attaining unto the true faith through that Holy Name, the very Jewel of Wonder.

When the new birth through the clearness of the Divine Promise is attained in the Eternal Kingdom, it is not like unto the birth of this world; then is there no inferiority even in those that in this world were sinners, for they have entered into Paradise.

The Holy Name of the Buddha of that Boundless Light that shineth into all the worlds of the Ten Regions, and the glory of His Wisdom, destroy the darkness of ignorance in the Eternal Night, thus fulfilling all the desires of men.

CONCERNING UNRIGHTEOUS DEEDS

These three things are expounded unto us by Donran Daishi. First, that faith is not holiness, for faith is not abiding. At one time it abides, at another it is gone.

And second: This faith is not Single Minded, for it hath not resolution.

And third: It continues not, for the other thoughts of the heart divide it against itself.

The three ways of this faith lead the one to the other one. On this must the believer fix his eyes. If his faith is not in holiness, then hath he not the faith of resolution.

And having not the faith that is resolute, that faith cannot endure, and because it endures not, how can he attain unto the faith of determination? And attaining not unto the faith of determination, the faith is not sanctified in him.

For the attainment of Right Practice expounded by the Master of the Written Word is according unto the true faith and this alone.

If a man return into the Great Way of the Divine Promise, eschewing the narrow ways of deeds and works, in him shall the true light of Nirvana be made manifest.

The mighty king So, he of the Ryo line, worshipped the Great Teacher Donran Daishi, naming him the Bodhisattva of Ran, turning his face in worship unto the dwelling-place of his Teacher.

CONCERNING DOSHAKU-ZENJI

Having cast away from him all trust in the righteous deeds of the sages, Doshaku-Zenji, the Great Teacher, hath taught us to enter in at the only gate that is the Gospel of the Pure Land.

Having thus cast away from him the laborious study of the Doctrine of Nirvana, Doshaku, the Great Teacher, himself trusted only in the power of the Divine Promise, and he persuaded men to follow after him.

In this world of sin that is so far removed from the blessed day of our Lord, is there no man who attains unto the wisdom Supreme, yea, not though he should compass all righteous doing. So teaches our Lord of Great Teaching.

He who succeeded unto the teaching of Donran-Daishi, Doshaku-zenji, the Great Priest, thus declares: "To toil and labor after righteous deeds in this life is the unavailing toil of self-effort."

In this world, the doing of evil and the sin that is wrought of men is violent and furious as the storm wind and rain. Therefore have the compassionate Buddhas exhorted men to seek their refuge within the Land of Purity.

From him that sins, throughout his life shall the fetters of illusion fall away, if he shall recite the Holy Name with love and adoration.

That he might lead men into the Eternal Kingdom—those men who are in this life fast bound unto the evil thing, our Father teaches us, saying, "Recite my name," and hath promised further, "Doing this, if they be not born again, I myself will not attain unto Wisdom."

CONCERNING ZENDO-DAISHI

Rising like unto an incarnation of the Mighty Ocean, Zendo, the great teacher, came into the world.

And for the sake of mankind in this sinful place, he called unto all the Buddhas of the Ten Regions to be his testimony unto his commentary on the Sutra.

Two interpreters of Zendo-Daishi were there in the age that followed his own, and these were Hoshō and Shōkō. They, it is, who have opened the Treasury of teaching that the inward purpose of the Blessed One should be wholly made known.

How should women turn their hearts unto wisdom—they who are fast bound with the five fetters? No, not through the ages of myriads of Kalpas, until they seek refuge in the Divine Promise of Him who is mighty.

Having thrown open the Gate of Righteousness, our Lord hath instructed mankind in every sort of righteous deed. He hath set before us how the five right deeds differ from the confused deeds that are outside the Five, so that mankind may enter the way of the Sole Practice.

To mingle the right action with the action that is not akin to it is called the confused practice. The man that errs therein hath not attained unto the single heart. He knows not thankfulness for the grace of the Enlightened One.

If he entreat in prayer the good things of this world, even though he recite only the Blessed Name, he is condemned therein, being also a man of the confused practice. He shall not be born into the Land of Purity.

Not one, indeed, but not far asunder are the confused deed and the confused practice. The teachings that are not the teachings of the Land of Purity are to be condemned as confused deeds.

Having invoked the testimony of all the Buddhas, Zendo-Daishi hath set before us the story of the two rivers, the one, the river of fire, the other the river of water, that he might incline the heart to righteous deeds, and guard the true faith of the Divine Promise.

Verily a simple man may attain unto the true Illumination, if he believe the Holy Promise that is the spirit of the teaching of Shinshu. Because for this only was the Lord made manifest in this world, and not according to those other teachings which shall pass away and be no more.

Before the Almighty Power of the Divine teaching do all the fetters of evil deeds fall away. Therefore is the Divine Promise of our Father invoked as that Holy Thing which giveth unto us omnipotent strength.

Yet, to whomsoever would enter the Promised Land, created in the power of His Divine Vow, is belief in his own strength impotent.

And because they are needless, therefore the wise who have received the Great and Lesser Vehicles must trust unto the promise of the Almighty One.

Whoso hath known himself the slave of illusion shall yet, relying on the Power of the Holy Promise, enter into the immortal joy of the Truth, and all his earthly body shall fall from him.

Merciful and compassionate parents unto us are the Blessed One and the Lord Buddha. For they have opened before us the ways of good, having so purposed that the great Faith shall be.

He who is one with the True Soul hath attained unto a heart clear and hard as diamond. Therefore is he at one with that man who hath the three excellent forms of Penitence. This hath the Great Teacher shown us.

By that faith alone, like unto a jewel of price, we who in this sinful world have our being, may enter into the Eternal Kingdom, being eternally freed from the yoke of birth and death.

At that moment when faith in the Enlightened One is perfected, pure and lasting as the diamond, then shall the Spiritual Light shine upon us and guard us, the light which forever guides us from rebirth and death.

Whoso attains not unto the True Faith hath not in him one of the Trinity of Virtues, that are Sincerity, Faith, and Hope, and the man that hath not one of these three holds not the perfect faith.

Whoso attains unto the True Faith given of Him is freed from all let and hindrance, for his heart is at one with the Divine Promise, and he is obedient unto the true teaching that is the Very Word of the Buddha.

Whoso hath comprehended the truth of the Holy Name is at that very moment freed from doubt. He hath possessed the Right thought, and he is commended as excellent and rare in his attainment.

He shall be let and hindered that is not at one with the Divine Promise, and therefore he whose faith is not full of Peace is a man who holds not the Divine Thought.

The attainment of the Divine Wisdom shall come unto him who recites the Holy Name, for his faith cometh from the Divine Promise of Him that leadeth him into the Promised Land. He shall not fail to attain unto the Great Nirvana.

At this time when the five Signs of Degeneration are manifest, many men are there who doubt and blaspheme the Holy Doctrine. Yea, even the Priests, together with the people, are enemies unto him who walketh in the right way.

He who blasphemes the Divine Promise is a man born blind. He shall sink into three evil worlds for age-long myriads of Kalpas.

Though the way into the Land that is in the West hath been made plain before us, yet the age-long Kalpas have rolled away without good fruit thereof, for we have hindered ourselves and our brethren that we might not enter therein.

Without the Almighty Strength of the Divine Promise how should we leave this sinful world? Wherefore we should live in hearty thanksgiving for the Grace of our Father, thinking ever upon the ocean deeps of his love.

For it is by the marvelous mercy of our Lord that we may cast aside the anguish of birth and death, in the shining hope of our Eternal Kingdom.

Therefore should we return unto the Lord righteous deeds in thanksgiving for His grace and mercy.

CONCERNING GENSHIN-SOZU

Genshin the Great Teacher declares:

"In this world have I, even I, appeared as an incarnation of the Buddha, and now, my work of Salvation being accomplished, I return unto the Eternal Kingdom that is my home.

From the teaching of our Lord hath Gen-shin, the Great Teacher, tenderly opened unto us the gate of the Doctrine of the Holy Name, and hath so taught mankind in this evil world that is far removed from the Golden Day of our Lord.

Genshin-Sozu, he who sat in the Assemblage on the Peak of Vultures in the time of our Lord, hath taught us that there are two Paradises, that which is eternal and that which is temporal, and thus sets forth the merit and the defect of the Right Practice and of the Mingled Deed.

Acharya Genshin, the Great Teacher, considering one of the Sutra with the commentary of Ekanzenji, hath made plain the attributes of the Land of Outermost Places.

For he said: "Not one man is there of thousands who may not be born into the Land of Purity." And thus saying, he commends the followers of the Right Practice.

And again:

"There is not even one among tens of thousands who may enter it." And so saying, he condemns the doers of the mingled deed.

Further he sets forth how few are the men who can enter into the True Land of Purity. And very solemnly he warns us that more are they that are born into the Temporal Paradise.

Wheresoever men or women, be they noble or lowly born, recite the Holy Name of our Father, there is no pre-eminence of place or time. Freely may they do this, whether walking, resting, sitting, or lying.

Though our eyes are so blinded by illusion that we discern not the light whereby He embraces us, yet that great mercy forever shineth upon us and is not weary.

Whatsoever may be his Visible Deed that would be born into the Promised Land, he shall not forget day or night to hold fast unto the name of the Divine Promise.

To us that in this world are sinners most sinful, there is none other way of Salvation save that we should enter into the Land of Purity, by reciting the holy name of Him who is our Father.

CONCERNING HONEN SHONIN

Since the day when Hōnen Shōnin appeared in the world, and set forth the single Ark of the Divine Promise, hath the Doctrine of the Pure Land gloriously shone upon the hearts of all men in the land of Nihon.

For from the strength of the wisdom of light, Hōnen, the Great Teacher, came into the world and hath taught the chosen doctrine of the Divine Promise, and he hath built Jodo-Shinshu upon the rock.

Though Zendo and Genshin, those great teachers, have well instructed us, yet had Hōnen Shōnin kept silence, wherewith should we know the holy teaching of Shin-Shu, we who dwell in remote country and in an evil day?

Throughout the long, long Kalpas of my lives that are over-past could I never find the way of Deliverance, and if Hōnen Shōnin, the Great Teacher, had not arisen in this world, vainly had I spent the precious hours of my life.

When his years were but fifteen, Hōnen Shōnin entered into the Way of Illumination, for in departing from worldly life he fulfilled his heart's desire, and by him was clearly understood the doctrine of the transience of life.

The excellent righteousness of Hōnen Shōnin, his deeds and the wisdom that was in him, drew unto him for refuge many even of chief priests of the heretics that seek Nirvana through the way of the sages. Yea, they sought him even as their appointed teacher, radiant and stray of soul as the diamond.

Even while Hōnen Shōnin yet walked in this world, there issued from his body rays of a golden shining, and this, so it is said, hath Kanezane Fujiwara beheld with his own eyes.

The people passed it from mouth to mouth that this Hōnen Shōnin was the living incarnation of Doshaku Zenji, or yet again of Zendo Daishi.

Before the eyes of men Hōnen Shōnin stood as the Boddhisattva of Wisdom, or, yet more, as the Blessed One again made flesh.

The Emperor and all his ministers did homage unto him, yea, and the men of the chief city and of the far countries.

He who had been Emperor, in the time of Jokyu, brought homage to Hōnen Shōnin. All the priests and scholars of the word of Confucius had understanding of the doctrine of Shin Shu.

A chosen vessel of the Blessed One that men might be saved, Hōnen Shōnin was manifested in the world, and he opened wide the gate of perfect wisdom, having instructed mankind in the Holy Faith.

Of all rare things it is the rarest that we should ourselves meet with the True Teacher, yet verily the chain of doubt in the Divine Mercy is the true cause of unending birth and death.

Hōnen Shōnin issued forth from the mysterious Light and his disciples beheld it. In his eyes was there naught of disparity between the wise and them that know not, between the noble and the lowly born.

And now, his time being at hand, Hōnen Shōnin spoke:

"Thrice have I taken birth in the Land of Purity, and of these three times the last hath given unto me the fullness of peace."

Once did Hōnen Shōnin speak, saying:

"In the glorious day of our Lord was I among the holy Assemblage on the Peak of Vultures, and my Spirit was rapt in self-instruction and in the doctrine of salvation."

Having taken birth in that small and remote island, Hōnen Shōnin spread abroad the doctrine of the Holy Name for the sake of all men's salvation. And thus had he done not only then, but many times in ages gone by.

That Buddha, whose light is infinite, was made flesh in this world as Hōnen Shōnin, and when his merciful work was accomplished, he returned into the Land of Purity.

When his life was drawing to a close, light was manifested about him as a cloud of glory, yea, and music of the heavenly places, sweet and excelling in harmony, and sweet odors scattered about him.

Following steadfastly after the ensample of the Nirvana of the Lord, he laid himself upon his right side, his head inclined unto the north, his face turned unto the west. And the crowding people attended upon him, even the priests and men and women of the nobles and of the lowly born.

Now the time when Hōnen Shōnin departed from this life was the twenty-fifth day of the young spring. In the second year of Kenriyaku he returned in peace unto the Land of the Father.

On the ninth day of February and the second of Ko-Yen, the revelation that here follows was sent unto me in a dream of morning.

It is necessary that men should believe the divine promise of Him who is Infinite.

Whoso believeth shall attain unto Perfect Wisdom, by the virtue of that Light which embraces him and shall never forsake him.

OF THE THREE PERIODS

Two thousand years and yet more are departed since the day when our Lord entered into Nirvana. Ended are the two glorious periods—the orthodox and the representative. Lament, O ye disciples, who in this closing age would follow after the Lord.

The teachings of our Lord have entered into the Dragon Palace, for in this closing age they are too high for men. Men are impotent to follow after their practice or to attain unto them.

Throughout the three periods hath the Divine Promise of the Buddha of Infinite Light prospered and grown. But in this period of the closing age all righteous deeds are hidden within the Dragon Palace.

In a certain Sutra are we thus instructed, since the age that now is a part of the fifth in this closing age wherein men are fast bound in warfare, all righteous deeds have disappeared from the world.

Since the ancient days the life of men, whose age counted as 80,000 years, hath declined and lessened. And when they could live but 20,000 years, they were men living in an evil world, and with the five signs of degeneration upon them.

And since time itself hath decayed, the bodily frame of man hath waxed smaller and feebler, and they are as furious serpents or as wicked dragons, for the decay of time worketh within them.

The illusion that is bred of ignorance increases, and is driven over the world like dust. Hatred great and unbreakable as the high mountains is in the stead of love.

The perversity of man is as strong and piercing as the thorn of the jungle. With eyes of suspicion and venomous anger do they accuse and persecute them who believe upon the Holy Name.

It is a mark of the degeneration of time that man's life is brief and death cometh upon him early and with iron hands breaks up his body and that which surrounds him wherein he dwelleth. And they who leaving justice turn to wickedness do destroy one another by their evil deeds.

No hope is there that the men now living in these last days shall escape the fetters of birth and death if they refuse the merciful promise of the Blessed One.

Of heretics in the faith are there ninety sorts that defile the world and only the teaching of the Enlightened One cleans it. By him alone that attains unto wisdom shall true joy to man be fulfilled according to nature and in peace.

In these last times of decay the priests, together with the people, do evil unto him that trusts in the doctrine of the Holy name.

Whoso attains not unto wisdom is eager to harm that man who, with single heart, accepted the exalted promise. There is no end to the infinity of the ocean of birth and death for those men who raven to destroy the doctrine that is mighty to save them if they would have it so.

Though the days of our present time are those that are called orthodox, we, in whom ignorance is fulfilled, have not within us the heart that is pure and true. How, then, can we of our own help attain unto the deeds that shall gain the wisdom that is made perfect.

The strong heart that is able to attain unto wisdom by self-help is beyond human knowledge and speech. How is it possible that men full of ignorance, fettered unto birth and death, should possess such a heart.

Though we were masters of the strong will of self-effort, even should we have seen face to face the Buddhas, myriad as the sands of Ganges—they who in this world were manifested the one after the other, yet were we drifted on the torrent of birth and death, in self-effort were no rescue for us.

In these sinful days that are called the representative and last times all the teachings of the Lord Buddha, the Sakiya-Muni have vanished away, but the Divine Promise of the Buddha of Infinite Light, shining greatly over the world, prosperously leads mankind unto the Eternal Kingdom.

After choice that is peerless and beyond the world's understanding, after five Kalpas of musing, the Blessed One built up the Divine Promise of the Light and Life Infinite. And this is the Essence of His Mercy showed upon us.

The noble mind that shall attain unto wisdom in the doctrine of the Pure Land is the mind that fain would become Buddha, and it is named: "The mind that shall save men who suffer."

The mind that shall save men is that mind given by the high promise of the Blessed One. Whoso attains unto the faith He giveth shall be lord of the great Nirvana.

Whoso attains unto the mind that would fain become Buddha, having sought refuge in the gift of the Blessed One, hath no term in his own gift of welfare to mankind, having forever laid down all self-righteousness.

According to the all-seeing promise of the Blessed One when the water of the faith He giveth enters the soul, illusion passes straight away into wisdom through the virtue of that true land of the Divine Promise.

That man who trusts in the two gifts granted by the Buddha of Infinite Light, is raised up into the sphere of the Lesser Enlightenment, and thence hath he the heart that dwelleth always on the perfection of the Blessed One.

He that attains unto the faith that is true gift of the promise of wisdom from the Blessed One, cometh unto the sphere of the Lesser Enlightenment, for he is embraced in the arms of the spiritual light that is of the Father Eternal.

Fifty-six thousand and seventy years shall pass before the Bodhisattva that is Maitreya shall attain unto the Perfected Wisdom. But whoso embraces the true faith shall at this very time be lord of the great Enlightenment.

He that hath ascended unto the height of the Lesser Enlightenment, accepting the Divine Promise of the Holy Name, shall enter into the Great Nirvana, being made equal unto the Bodhisattva Maitreya.

He that receives the true Faith, and is one with them that return no more to birth and death, shall receive the Perfected Wisdom, even as that Bodhisattva Maitreya that is called, "He that shall come."

And the wise in the age which is called Representative, having utterly renounced all the doctrine of self-dependence, have entered in at the gate of the Holy Name. For this is the way chosen for that Age.

He who recites the Holy Name, having attained unto the true faith, shall unceasingly adore the Eternal Father, that he may make a return unto Him for His Grace.

Inexplicable and unutterable merit shall be given unto him who, living in this sinful world, believeth the Divine Promise that proceeds from His will.

For the true welfare of men that shall be the Buddha of the Great Light hath given the holy name of Wisdom unto the Bodhisattva of Wisdom.

And with great compassion for mankind in this evil world the Bodhisattva of Wisdom persuades them to believe upon the Holy Name, and sweetly welcomes the believer that he may lead him into the Land of Purity.

By the mercy of our Lord and of the Blessed One we are able to attain unto the heart that desires Buddhahood. At that time alone, when we enter into the wisdom of the faith, shall we be ourselves like unto them that would return good unto the Buddha for His Grace.

It is by the strength of the Divine Promise that we can reach unto the holy name of Wisdom. Without the wisdom of the faith, how is it possible that we should attain unto the Nirvana?

The Divine Light shineth over the Deep Night of ignorance, therefore sorrow not that the wisdom of your eyes is darkened. The holy Ark is at hand that voyages over the great ocean of birth and death ; therefore fear not because your sin is heavy.

Great as is the night of the Divine Promise of our Salvation, so light is the heaviest of our sins. Immeasurable is the wisdom of our Father, and therefore they that are strong, as also they that weary, shall never be forgotten.

Our Father hath perfected His mercy by uttering the Divine Promise that giveth all His merit unto man, that He might save them that are fast bound unto birth and death.

Yea, the recitation of His Holy Name is given of the Blessed One. Therefore we must not offer this unto Him for the acquirement of merit. For this will He most surely disdain.

Yea, verily, when the water of the mind of man flows into the great Ocean of the Divine Promise of the Perfect Wisdom it is changed and becometh the mind of infinite compassion.

And the Lord saith, speaking through a certain Sutra:

"My disciples that shall be, they that are sinners because of the lost way and love of evil things, it is they that shall destroy my holy doctrine."

Whoso blasphemes the doctrine of the Holy Name shall suffer without ceasing, for he shall fall into the depth of the Hell of Avichi for eighty thousands of Kalpas.

He to whom is given the true entrance into the True and Promised Land, by the grace of our Lord and of the Blessed One, shall be one with those men who return no more unto birth and death, and after this transitory life attain unto the Great Peace.

Well may we understand from the teaching of the myriad Buddhas in the Ten Regions—they that protect mankind—that the strong mind that seeks enlightenment by self-effort is vain and impotent.

The Buddhas in the Ten Regions, innumerable as the sands of Ganges, bear witness that very few are there of men in this sinful world and decaying time that attain unto the true faith.

If we accept not the two divine gifts, the gift of entering the Promised Kingdom, and the gift of return into this evil world, then shall the wheel of birth and death turn with us forever. And how shall we endure to sink into the sea of suffering?

Whoso believeth the marvelous wisdom of that Blessed One, shall be joined unto them that return no more unto birth and death. And when, possessed of excelling knowledge, such a man is born into Paradise, soon shall he attain unto the Perfected Wisdom.

It is the sole way unto the Promised Land that man should believe the wisdom that is beyond human knowledge, of the Enlightened One. Yet it is of all hard things hardest to attain unto the Faith, the true way that leadeth to Paradise.

Casting aside the sorrow of birth and death, that sorrow which is timeless in its beginning, I hope now solely for the Great Nirvana. There is no end to my thankfulness for the two mighty gifts of our Eternal Father.

Few are the believers that shall be born into the Land that is promised, but many are they that shall be born into the Temporal Paradise. Because the hope that we shall see Light by our own strength is vain, having no foundation, we have therefore drifted on the ocean of birth and death for many myriads of Kalpas.

Because in the gift of the Holy Name is a grace great and wonderful, if man attain unto the gift of departing, that of itself shall guide him unto the gift of returning.

Through the great mercy of the gift of departing shall we attain unto the compassion of the gift of returning. If it were not the free gift of the Blessed One, how should we attain unto wisdom in the Land of Purity.

The Buddha of the Infinite Light, together with the Bodhisattvas of Compassion and Wisdom, having taken the Ark of the Divine Promise, that is voyaging on the ocean of birth and death, have gathered and saved mankind therewith.

Whoso in heart and soul believeth the Divine Promise of the Buddha of Infinite Light must diligently recite the Holy Name both sleeping and waking.

Those men in the hierarchy of Sages that have trusted unto self-effort for the means of attaining wisdom, on entering into the heritage of the Divine Promise believe in it as in the reason that transcends all reason.

Though the teachings of the Lord stand for ever, yet unto none is it possible to follow them in exactness, and therefore is there none that may attain unto supreme enlightenment in these last days of the falling away.

In India, in China, and the land of Japan, may the many teachers of the doctrine of the Land of Purity, with compassion and tender acceptance, persuade mankind to strive unto the true faith that they may be joined unto those that return no more unto birth and death.

Even as His friends the Lord commends those men that, having attained unto the true faith taught of the Blessed One unto us, dwell within the joy of holiness.

It is very meet that our souls rejoice exceedingly in the grace of the great compassion of the Buddha. Yea, even to the extinction of the body. And for the gracious giving of our spiritual teachers we must in like manner rejoice, yea, though our very bones be broken.

CONCERNING BELIEF AND DOUBT

Whoso comprehends not the wisdom of the Enlightened One, and doubts concerning His illumination, shall rise no higher than the Outermost Places, for he hath trusted in the power of Reward, and hath relied upon the principle of morality.

Whoso doubts the wisdom of the Enlightened One—that wisdom beyond all human understanding—and recites the Holy Name, trusting in the merit of himself, shall not rise beyond the outermost bounds of the Pure Land that is the Temporal Paradise, for he hath not the grace of right thankfulness for His Compassion.

Whoso shall accept the doctrine of rewards and doubts the wisdom of Him that hath Light that surpasses all knowledge of man, shall be made captive in Doubting Castle, and the three jewels of the faith shall no more be his.

For his sin, in that he hath doubted the wisdom of the Enlightened One, shall he remain in the Outermost Places of the Land of Purity. And for as much as we are taught that the sin of doubt is grievous, we are also instructed that he must there dwell for many Kalpas.

If the prince commits a sin against his Father, even the Chakravarti, the King, he is fettered as a prisoner, though the chain be of gold.

Whoso recites the Holy Name, and so doeth as a work of self-merit, shall be bound in the prison of the sevenfold gems, for he believeth not right by the divine promise of that Holy One, and heavy is the sin of his doubting.

Yet he even that hath a doubting soul and sins the sin of self-merit, must needs strive to comprehend the merciful goodness of the Blessed One, and he shall recite the Holy Name if he would at all be equal unto him that holds the true faith.

It is the Law that he who soweth shall reap what he soweth, therefore the man that is full of righteous deeds for the sake of self-merit shall enter into the prison of the sevenfold gems, for he doubts the marvelous wisdom of Him that hath the Light.

Whoso doubts of the wisdom of Him that hath Light beyond the imagining of man, and trusts to the root of goodness and virtue—he shall not attain unto the Soul of Great Mercy, for he is born into the Outermost Places of Paradise, and slow and dull of heart is he.

Among those men that doubt the Holy Word, some are imprisoned in the shut bud of the Lotus. And they shall be despised as they that in illusion are born into the outermost Paradise or are held captive within the narrow walls of the womb.

Whoso doubts the omniscience of the wisdom of the Light-Bearer, but holds to his belief in Reward, excellent ofttimes in making the root of goodness to grow,

Because he doubts the wisdom of the Eternal Wisdom, and is held captive as in the strait prison of the womb, hath neither knowledge nor wisdom, and is compared unto a man straightly bound in captivity.

He that is born into the outermost place, all glorious with the sevenfold jewels, shall not in five hundred years behold that threefold jewel, the Triratna, for there is in him no spiritual well-doing, that he should give it unto his fellow-men.

To him who is born into the Palace, glorious with the seven jewels, for five hundred years there shall befall many sorts of sorrows from his own evil doing.

Whoso hopes reward and makes to flourish the root of goodness, shall remain in the transitory Paradise, for though he be a good man, yet hath he a doubting heart.

Because he accepts not the Divine Promise of Him who is the Light unspeakable, and carries his doubt with him unto Paradise, therefore the shut flower of his heart opens not, therefore is he unshapen as a child in the womb.

When he perceives the Land of Purity, the Bodhisattva Maitreya thus questions the Holy One, saying, "What is the cause and what the circumstance of that man who, having been born, yet remains as it were straitened in the womb?

And thus spoke the Lord unto the Bodhisattva Maitreya saying, "Whoso trusts in the root of goodness that he himself makes to grow and hath a doubting soul, he it is that is in the outermost places of the Paradise, he it is that is said to be straightened still in the womb of ignorance."

He who doubts the wisdom of Him that is all Light, shall for his sin be made captive until five hundred years be gone, and this is called the conception within the womb of ignorance.

Whoso doubts the wisdom that is beyond man's understanding, and hath believed the doctrine of reward, shall of a certainty be born within Doubting Castle, and this is called conception within the womb of ignorance.

Whoso trusts upon self-righteousness rather than upon the wisdom of the Enlightened One that is beyond man's knowledge, shall be conceived within the womb of ignorance, and to him shall the mercy of the Three Jewels be unknown.

Whoso doubts the wisdom of the Enlightened One that surpasses all knowledge of man and trusts in the hope of reward, and would attain unto birth in Paradise by making the root of goodness to grow, shall be straightened in the womb of ignorance.

Heavy is the sin of doubting the wisdom of the Buddha. He who is instructed taketh refuge in the wonderful wisdom of the Enlightened One, being in contrition for his foolishness.

These twenty-three psalms above-written are made by me that men should know the heaviness of their sin in doubting the Divine Promise of the Buddha of Infinite Light.

IN PRAISE OF PRINCE SHOTOKU

Through the compassion of Shotoku the great prince we, having accepted the Divine Promise sprung from the unsearchable wisdom of the Illuminated One, are made equal unto Maitreya. Bodhisattva—the Buddha that shall be—having been united unto those men who return no more to birth and death.

The mighty Bodhisattva of Compassion, he who is the Savior, was made manifest in this world as Shotoku the Prince, who, like a father, hath not forsaken us, and like a mother is ever amongst us.

From that past where was no beginning until the day that now is, hath Shotoku the great prince, the Compassionate, dwelt among us like unto a father and a mother.

Shotoku the Prince, from his Compassion, hath persuaded us to enter in at the Divine Promise of the wondrous wisdom of the Light-Bearer. And through this are we joined unto those men who return no more unto birth and death.

Whoso attains unto the holy faith that is the power of divinity, must, in the Ten Regions of the world, find the twofold gift of the Enlightened One, that he may live in thankfulness for His grace.

Shotoku, he who is mercy's self, the Compassionate, he who is like unto a father, and the Bodhisattva of Mercy, the divine tenderness, his succor is merciful as the pity of a mother.

Testimony is there that Shotoku the prince hath mercy upon us, from the myriads of Kalpas even unto this day, because the wondrous wisdom of Him who is Light bears the load of his debt for the believer.

Therefore before the eyes of His wisdom is the evil as the good, the pure as the unclean.

Shotoku, the Prince, he that is in Japan called the Lord of Teaching, he whose great mercy overtops all spoken words of gratitude, must we therefore praise for evermore, having with single heart sought refuge in him.

He who hath pitied the dwellers in the lands of Japan, the Prince of Jogu, he whose ways are merciful, hath spread abroad the Divine Promise of the Enlightened One. Therefore let us praise him with great rejoicing. Throughout the many myriads of Kalpas, birth after birth fell hitherto upon us.

We to whom he showed forth his compassion must be swift to praise him, having continually sought refuge in him, and with a single mind.

The high Prince Shotoku, he who hath guarded us and with great carefulness led us upwards from remotest times, hath lovingly entreated us to seek our refuge in the two-fold gift of the Enlightened One.

WHEREIN WITH LAMENTATION I MAKE MY CONFESSION

Though I seek my refuge in the true faith of the Pure Land,

Yet hath not mine heart been truly sincere.

Deceit and untruth are in my flesh,

And in my soul is no clear shining.

In their outward seeming are all men diligent and truth speaking,

But in their souls are greed and eager and unjust deceitfulness,

And in their flesh do lying and cunning triumph.

Too strong for me is the evil of my heart. I cannot overcome it.

Therefore is my soul like unto the poison of serpents,

Even my righteous deeds, being mingled with this poison, must be named the deeds of deceitfulness.

Shameless though I be and having no truth in my soul,

Yet the virtue of the Holy Name, the gift of Him that is enlightened,

Is spread throughout the world through my words being as I am.

There is no mercy in my soul.

The good of my fellow-man is not dear in mine eyes. If it were not for the Ark of Mercy, the divine promise of the Infinite Wisdom,

How should I cross the Ocean of Misery?

I, whose mind is filled with cunning and deceit as the poison of reptiles, am impotent to practice righteous deeds.

If I sought not refuge in the gift of our Father, I should die the death of the shameless.

It is a token of this evil age that in this world the priests, together with the people,

In secret serve strange gods,

While bearing the appearance of the devout sons of Buddha.

Sad and corrupt is it that the priests and people, following after the superstitions of auspicious times and days, seek sooth-saying and festivals

And worship the gods of heaven and earth.

Though I have heard that the names of priest and monk are honorable,

Yet now are they held as light as the five shameless precepts of Devadatta.

Being of one accord with the many minds of the heathen,

They bow in worship before devils,

While yet wearing the robe of the Buddha.

Sad and sorrowful is it that all the priests and people now in the land of Yamato should worship the devils of heaven and earth, in the name of the holy mysteries of the Buddha.

It is a mark of the downward way of this evil age that men despise the name of priest or monk as a mean thing, considering them like unto slaves.

May they yet bring offerings with homage unto the priests, even as you do unto Saliputra or Mahamonugalyayana, those two great servants of the Lord; though they are priests but in name and without discipline, for this is the time of degeneration and of the last days.

Though sin hath no substance in itself, and is but the shadow of our illusion, and soul is in itself pure, yet in all this world is there no sincere man.

Great sorrow is it that, in the wicked world of this age now so near its end, the high priests who are born in the palankin, and the monks who bear it now in Nara and Mount Hiyei, desire high secular rank as the greatest honor.

That they consider the monk and nun as their slaves, and mock at the honorable title of priest and minister, even as at the mean name of slave, gives testimony that they despise the teaching of the Buddha.

These sixteen psalms written above are written by me, Gutoku, with lamentation, to be a record. To me even the honorable priests and monks of the Central Temples seem now to be despised.

ADDITIONAL PSALMS

Having fulfilled forty and eight of the Divine Promise,

He attained unto the supreme enlightenment, and was manifest as the Buddha of Infinite Light.

Whoso seeks refuge with Him shall be certainly born into the Land of Purity.

Into the Promised Land—the Paradise of the Great Calm.

He who practices the righteous deeds of the mingled motive hath no claim of birth,

Therefore He that is Infinite would have us follow the deeds of the single practice that is chosen of Him as teaching that is at the root.

The merit of His holy austerities throughout the myriads of Kalpas is fully declared in his name of Amida (the Infinite).

And the Holy Name, after the consideration of five Kalpas,

Will be accorded unto us who are alive in this degenerated age.

Because action, speech, and mind of the Infinite Life and the believer in the Holy Name are welded as into a diamond, therefore shall he certainly be one with the men that return no more unto birth and death.

He that hath much knowledge and keeps the Pure Land is not chosen,

And whoso breaks the Holy Law and sins is not disdained.

Only he that seeks refuge in the Eternal Father shall enter into Buddhahood as a pebble is transmuted into gold.

Our faith that endures as the diamond cometh from the mind of the Buddha that eternally endures.

Lacking the aid of the Divine Power, how should we attain unto the unchanging mind?

In the great ocean of the Divine Promise

Is there no ripple of illusion.

If we enter into the ark of the Holy Vow,

The spirit of mercy shall take part with our self-endeavor.

Since we have believed the Divine Promise,

How is it possible we should be in the power of life or death?

Unchanged may be our sinful body,

But our heart is in the Paradise forever.

www.ingramcontent.com/pod-product-compliance
Lightning Source LLC
LaVergne TN
LVHW041634070426
835507LV00008B/626